AF265966

Written by Danielle Bradley

For Morgan,
my sunshine.
xo

And for Michelle-
thank you for showing me rainbows.

Illustrated by Ivy Trazsi

For Adrienn,
my best friend with a million colours.

The Rainbow Road
Canada

*My endless love and gratitude to
Matt, Angie, & Erica,
for your feedback, patience, and support.*

*Ten million thanks to Ivy,
without whom these words would be lifeless.*

Ten Million Colours
Copyright © Danielle Bradley 2024
Illustrations, design & cover © Ivy Trazsi 2024

No part of this publication may be reproduced in whole or in part, or stored in a retrieval system, or transmitted in any form or by any means, electronic, mechanical, photocopying, recording, or otherwise, without written permission of the publisher.

ISBN 978-1-0689894-1-4
ISBN 978-1-0689894-2-1 (ebook)

First edition, September 2024
Printed in Canada

Published by The Rainbow Road
www.therainbowroad.ca
heythere@therainbowroad.ca

It is estimated that the human eye can see...

Here is a rainbow, bold and bright,
where 7 colours soar,
and if we mix these colours,
we can find TEN MILLION more!

When blue and yellow meet, we see
a leaf,
a frog,
a tree.

A tortoise walking on green grass,
a turtle in the sea.

Blue and red together give us velvet indigo.
A fig,
a fish,
a butterfly.

A queen upon her throne.

Add some yellow to your red
and out jumps orange, bright!

A snowman's nose,

a tiger's tail,

a campfire in the night.

Mix a little
red in white —
what colour, do you think?

A pig,
a pearl,
a popsicle,

petunias –
all in pink!

A splash of green in yellow makes
a tangy twist of lime.

Red and orange together paint
a late vermilion sky.

Orange and yellow mix to make
a marigold or peach.

Teal is blue and green,
where lazy waves lie on the beach.

Violet blooms when red and purple dance around and 'round.

Blend them all together for

delicious chocolate brown!

Countless colours more, we find,
when adding **black** or **white**.
A little here, a smidgen there,
to make them dark or light.

Mint turns to

jade,

then **emerald**,

then **British**
racing green.....................

then pale
aquamarine.

peacock blue,

............while ocean fades to

A dash of this, a drop of that—
more colours being made!
Each time we try a different way,
we find another shade!

Like **navy blue**

and **amethyst**

and **lavender**

and **puce.**

Magenta,
coral,
apricot,
banana
and chartreuse.

Here's crimson,
scarlet,
amber,
dandelion,
tangerine.

Flamingo,

orchid,

periwinkle,

sage

and olive green.

The more we stir, the more we mix,
the more that we explore,
the more we see our colours turn to
many MILLIONS more!

Danielle Bradley is an early educator on a mission to ensure
childhood wellness across the globe!
Her stories encourage kindness, inclusivity, self-love, and discovery among children
(and their adults).

For future releases and childhood wellness resources, visit
www.therainbowroad.ca

www.ingramcontent.com/pod-product-compliance
Lightning Source LLC
Chambersburg PA
CBHW042130030726
47599CB00002B/427

* 9 7 8 1 0 6 8 9 8 9 4 1 4 *